CW01500013

First published in Great Britain in 2022 by JaJaJa Books

Text copyright © 2022 Multi-Schools Council

Design by Amanda Sebborn-Connelly

ISBN 9798364865878

- Autism, ADHD and Mental Health

We may all be different but
we have the same smile

DEDICATIONS

The book is written on behalf of the young people of Essex who are part of the Multi-School's Council.

I also want to dedicate this book to the late Kerris Emery, without whom there would never have been an opportunity to write this book. One of the amazing teachers.

Background

The Multi-Schools Council (MSC) started because a young girl called Charlie wanted to see more awareness of children's differences while attending school. Her message was clear: in special educational settings, most teachers and other children understand each other's needs, or at least accept them for who they are. However, children must leave these schools one day and many will go into mainstream society where others don't understand them.

This prompted us to create a Multi-Schools Council by bringing together children from different backgrounds and asking them how we could challenge negative perceptions of them. It started with four local schools holding a council-style meeting in North Essex and now includes the participation of over 400 schools across five separate local authorities. The children involved have helped put together the content for each section in this book, and everything that we do is driven by their ideas and thoughts.

This is a model which we know works for children and one we wish to build upon further so that children across the UK can benefit. We want children's views to be taken seriously, especially regarding their own needs. We may have a large amount of knowledge and skills from working with children, but nothing can replace lived experience. We want to show the Department for Education our work across different local areas and hope they also share our vision of ensuring that all children with Special Educational Needs and Disabilities (SEND) have a voice on an equal level to their peers. If we get this right, we could have MSC young leaders across the country and ensure that disability awareness starts to form part of our national curriculum.

When we speak to staff in schools, many of them agree with our children that more awareness and training is needed regarding children with SEND. Within our teacher training courses, although some content is covered, the amount of detail included compared with other areas is very minimal. This is not right. The same can be said for mental health teams working in schools, and the training to prepare them: where is the specific content for working with children who may have autism or ADHD? We hope to address this in our book by giving more detail.

However, all the sessions on which we base this book are only an hour long on average, and to cover such detailed subjects in that time is difficult. We are only touching the surface, and effort should be made to follow up on the understanding and strategies provided. Importantly, what we feel comes through is the way our children have influenced the book with real-life examples of what can either support them or potentially be difficult.

Overview – What this book includes

How to talk about SEND with children – This section focuses on how you might deliver a whole school assembly or a classroom activity.

Autism awareness – This section focuses on understanding autism, while suggesting useful strategies that can be put in place in school settings.

ADHD awareness. Part one – This section takes a deep look into ADHD while discussing common challenges and strategies of support.

ADHD awareness. Part two – This section looks more specifically at how you might explain ADHD to a younger person.

Mental health in schools – This section explores early intervention strategies and the idea of building resilience in young people.

Useful links – A short section on useful links and further reading

How to talk about SEND with children
<u>Talking about our differences</u>

The starting point when discussing SEND awareness is not being scared to talk about our differences. So, within our SEND assemblies we ask children of all ages to firstly consider what 'special educational needs' actually means to them. This is an opener for you to try in your own school setting. To then help explain children's differences, the best way we have found is to focus on the brain. To demonstrate this, we use a brain in the form of a plastic model and a long piece of string. We ask two children to hold the string taut in front of everyone, and a third child to hold the string halfway along. We then explain that every single child has at least one talent. Some children won't know what it is yet, and some might not want to admit it as it may not be cool enough, but they all have talents. I ask them to imagine taking their brains out of their heads and placing them somewhere along the piece of string. I then add more details about how some brains can think or work very differently. On the right-hand side of the string as the students look at it we have some children who don't use words to communicate because their brains don't work in this way; however, they may use sign language, or if they would like a drink, for example, they may show a picture of a drink. This is a clever way of adapting the use of their brain. In the middle of the line of string, the brains are what some people may describe as neurotypical; however, even within that area, children still learn, play and work in different ways. On the left-hand side of the string there are some children who will use lots of words to communicate, can remember lots of information and are potentially very literal learners; however, they may find loud noise a struggle, so they may wear ear defenders, or perhaps they don't like being around lots of people so they have a smaller group of friends. The point to make here is that no area of the line is better than the other, so it's not stupid or 'unstupid'. It's just different.

To emphasise this point, whilst we focus on the left-hand side of the string, I talk about a young boy who, if I asked him how to get from Colchester to Edinburgh, would be able to tell me every single road I would need to take, including all the B roads. Going to the right-hand side of the string, I describe a young girl who, if I told her that I was born on 23 October 1991, would be able to tell me what day of the week I was born on, and would be able to do that with anyone's birthday. This girl learnt some language skills over the years, so was not at the very end of the right-hand side; however, she was still not overly verbal in her communication. This does not mean everybody has autism or another learning difference, but it does mean all of our brains function differently.

Different schools

The next area we focus on is the difference between a special school and a mainstream school (terminology that we will revisit later). I ask the children: "What is a special school?" Normally, many of their responses include special school pupils' inability to learn or to cope with exams or their behaviour being bad. There are always negative connotations associated with their responses to these schools. We explain that children who go to these schools still learn English and maths, etc but may be taught in a slightly different way. This refers back to all our brains working differently, and people learning in different ways. Children still do exams where appropriate, they still have friends and still do real lessons, but it's all about the environment that the school creates. As a teacher, you can reflect on your own classroom and think about how you ensure all children's differences are accepted within that setting.

"Strength lies in differences, not in similarities."

<u>Our differences and showing kindness</u>
At this point, we ask the children to look at each other to see if they can identify the differences between them. I make the point that not every difference is one you can see. This ensures that we start to accept the things that make us unique, since we are human beings and not sheep! Sheep will follow the flock, whereas children should be proud of who they are and embrace their individual strengths. To close the assembly, I ask the children to consider how they can be kinder to each other, no matter what their differences are. It's summed up with another saying: "Be somebody who makes everybody feel like a somebody." The important messages from this assembly can be transferred into the classroom. An extension of what they have learnt previously is useful here. This could be by identifying positive

role models with disabilities, kindness pledges to one another, peer-to-peer self-esteem work or identifying their own strengths.

Autism awareness
What is autism?
The children I work with want us to write about autism because not enough people understand them, since people often see the condition before the person. Schools can sometimes be places that expect children to fit into a mould without really understanding individual qualities. We should accept children for who they are, not try to change them. This chapter talks about the understanding and strategies that children with autism themselves have suggested or used within a school environment. One thing we know is that when we don't get this right, the impact on children's mental health is significant. If we imagine going to work every day, not being able to communicate our needs, feeling as if we don't fit in and not always understanding the environment we are in, we can understand how children with autism might be feeling. These are the common messages we hear from the children we work with. What the chapter does not explore is the difficulties and time needed to obtain a

diagnosis, but we know that early diagnoses for any differences are crucial. However, just because a child doesn't have a diagnosis, we can still support them, as many of the strategies and ways of working below could benefit many children regardless of an autism diagnosis.

The next part of this book focuses on autism by building understanding and also looking at some positive strategies that you can use. The first point to make is that if you have met one child with autism, you have only met one child with autism. The focus here must be on getting to know an individual. For instance, can you list the things they really like? Often, with autism, children can have very particular interests (this does not mean all children with autism like trains!). Your challenge here is to consider their areas of interest and look at how you can get these themes into the everyday curriculum. For example, a child in your class may really enjoy various types of animals. So, within your English lessons, is there a way to link this interest to the topic you are studying? If we hook the child in early, they are more likely to engage, feel comfortable and make better educational progress. I appreciate a person-centred approach to every lesson is not always possible; however, once we get these things in place, it will not only help the individual but the rest of the class, too. Now, let's consider what autism means. We could spend hours coming up with a definition, but for ease, we shall use this:

"A developmental DISORDER of variable severity that is characterised by DIFFICULTY in social interaction and communication and by RESTRICTED or repetitive patterns of thought and behaviour." – The American Psychological Association

Whilst reading this, can you identify why three words are in block capitals? Hopefully you have identified that all three of these words are very negative, which unfortunately is how some people can view autism, but we like to look at things in another way.

If we take disorder first – obviously this is a health term used widely, but I like to look at it in a different way. Some children with autism really benefit from order and can place things in a particular way that works with their brain development. This is about building on the skills they may have rather than looking at the term disorder but using an approach that works for them.

When it comes to difficulty in social interactions, there may be times when this is true; however, there are interventions we can put in place to support it, and this comes back to the environment you create.

And finally, restricted – the question I put to school staff is whether these children are restricted or whether it is the restrictions that society places on them. The key here is to try and put ourselves in their shoes and see the world through their lens, which we are going to describe as part of this chapter.

"We are not neurotypical, but we still want an education"

Understanding autism further – Context
Something that many of us do every day is automatically make scripts and scenarios of things we see, hear and experience, etc. For example, we have a script or scenario of a bank robbery, a book, a TV show or a family member. This is done automatically because of the connections we make in our brains and the different social contexts that we understand. I now want us

to consider somebody who has autism – they can often see a context very differently, so, for example, their idea of what might happen in a restaurant may differ from other people. To go into even more detail, consider a young girl who comes home from school every day at 3.30 pm. At 3.40 pm this young girl's routine involves getting into the shower. One particular day, her parents have a plumber working in the bathroom where she showers. The young girl goes into the bathroom, turns on the shower and starts to undress even though the plumber is still there working. This young girl's context is that 3.40 pm equates to shower time. The fact there is somebody else in the bathroom too does not affect her context. You can see the difficulty this can present. Some people with autism can learn the context of a new situation, but this needs communicating on a level they understand and practice through learnt routines. We may also need to put an intervention in place, such as a social story. To expand on this further, another experience of a young girl I worked with involved a troubling time within school assemblies. At the end of each week, one child from our class would be given a star-of-the-week certificate in the assembly hall, in front of the other year groups, and it would be handed out by the head teacher. For the first two weeks of term, this young girl did not manage to achieve this certificate, which evoked a lot of anger. Her anger was not directed at the staff in our class, but rather at the head teacher. This young girl's context was that the head teacher handed out the certificates in the assembly hall. The girl did not understand the process of working throughout the week with the staff in the classroom, and then picking up on what she could do to achieve the certificate. We wrote a social story that explained the steps of how this young girl could achieve this certificate. The story needed to be personalised, so included pictures of her and her classroom, but it also explained how her peers were also part of this process, that is, they could also get the certificate some weeks! When using this technique, a social story needs to be read regularly to ensure there is a positive impact as we know some children with autism learn through repetition. In summary, this goes back to how we scaffold children's learning. We know there are certain steps when teaching a child a new strategy or concept and this will start to build connections in the brain. When scaffolding for children with autism, we need to try and put ourselves in their shoes and look through their lens. Autism as context blindness can make the world confusing and unpredictable, which is why strategies may need to be adapted or repeated until the context is understood.

Communication

We need to look at autism as being a spectrum (refer back to the SEND Assemblies section, which gives you an idea of how to talk about this spectrum). Some children with autism are very verbal and often able to remember lots of facts and information. Often, some children will benefit from lots of detail, so some suggestions here would be to have a visual timetable in the classroom or boards which focus on the here and now. Some children with autism benefit from their own visual timetables because they are more relatable, and they can remove an activity from their timetable, reminding them that it is finished. This fills the gaps that other children may just predict or assume, whereas with autism this can often be difficult. Whilst discussing communication, we also need to consider that some children with autism are very literal learners; so, for example, they may take the phrase "It's raining cats and dogs outside" literally. The point here is to ensure that, as teachers, we are aware of the language we use and reflect on words or phrases that may have a double-meaning or be rather abstract in their nature. A tool that speech and language therapists use is something called the Blank's

Levels of Questioning system, which is particularly useful for children with autism when understanding their language and communication skills. The system has different levels, enabling you to gauge where a child is on their communication journey. For example, Level 1 is a very basic level of understanding where you would not expect to use too many steps within a question, nor that a child would have an in-depth understanding of the question you pose, whereas at Level 4 a child would have a deeper understanding and you may be able to ask more probing multi-step questions. Each level has questions and suggestions of the ways you should approach language and communication for that child. The tool is simple and can be accessed by different educational professionals, and there are some links at the end of this book to help build your understanding.

The other side of the spectrum is where we may have some children who can be described as non-verbal; however, the term I tend to use is pre-verbal. The reasoning behind this is that I have worked with children who up to the age of double digits have not used verbal communication but then have begun to communicate verbally. We must, however, appreciate that, as human beings, verbal communication is not the only way we can interact. There are many communication tools out there. I particularly use the Picture Exchange Communication System (PECS) which is a picture tool that allows children to ask for a drink, go to the toilet and various other requests. We must also consider the use of technology in that many of these resources are available digitally and children are becoming increasingly more confident in using such technology. You may want to consider what technology you have in your schools, and how children with communication difficulties might be able to access it. Other strategies can include allowing children to draw, which can also develop into art or play therapy, or using the principles behind something such as Lego therapy, which is a great tool to help build communication skills. A key point to focus on is how you allow your children to express themselves.

The next part is really getting to know an individual, which is a theme throughout this book. When it comes to communication, this is so important because we need to observe and read body language and the pre-verbal sounds that children may make in different situations. Noises can be a way of expressing how a child is feeling. I always think back to when I was young in a supermarket and there may have been a child who was making loud noises and I didn't understand why this was. We need to explain these situations because, if we don't, that is when assumptions are made, and children become unsure about how to approach these situations. In a school setting, we should try and look at when these sounds happen – is it because of a change of environment or a change of activity? Is this a form of expression? Good practice here would be keeping notes of this communication, especially a one plan or an Educational Health Care Plan, so that the next teacher has a clear picture of the child.

Finally, consider how much information we give to children at once. Your starting point here is to reflect on the Blank's Levels system; however, let's break this down further. For some children, you may be able to say to them, for example: "Go to the kitchen, open the fridge and get out the orange juice," and they can process this instruction. However, some children may go to the kitchen and open the fridge, but the third request was just too much. We need to ensure that we are not overloading children with information and if we bring this back to the classroom, we can look at this in different subjects.

For example, a child in a maths lesson may get

a sheet of ten questions. I know of children for whom that would be too overwhelming. A simple strategy here is to cut these questions down and just give them to the child one at a time. This allows the child to see the questions in a more achievable manner. If we stick to these principles across other subjects, many children will feel less overwhelmed.

"I think, with our help, we can change the world" – MSC ambassador

Socialising
For the next part of this chapter, I want you to imagine the following situation:
1. You walk into a room which is full of people you don't know.
For some of you reading this book, you might already be feeling slightly uncertain.

2. The lights are bright, the food on the menu is seafood and the room is very loud and full of conversation.

3. One area of the room is hot, another is cold. You can't decide if you're going to keep your jacket on or take it off.

4. You can't read anyone's emotions. You walk around this room and you can't recognise if people are happy, sad, confused – you just don't know.

5. You don't understand some of the language used. You can almost imagine you are in a foreign country and you don't speak that language.

The question is, would you like to be in this situation? No alcohol is allowed as this can be a way that some adults may cope with a difficult situation – however, children don't have this option.

Let's consider each aspect of the scenario.
1. Assemblies. Where there is good practice, some children with autism can become comfortable in a classroom environment as they get used to the routines, objects and people. However, if we consider school assemblies, there are going to be many variables, including the environment, the people and different objects. The first strategy is to consider preparing our children for this change, so can you take a picture of that new environment, or can you make them aware of the people they will be around? Or are there some familiar objects in the assembly hall that they could relate to? For children who struggle in such an environment,

you may seat them at the end of assembly line, rather than directly in the middle, which can be quite overwhelming. At the end of the line, they'll be able to see the exits or a familiar person they have a good relationship with. You may even sit the child away from the assembly line so they can have a clearer picture of what is around them. The starting point is always to consult with the young person first. The final point is to consider how valuable that assembly or activity is for the child, so perhaps you build up to that assembly in manageable chunks before they can last the duration. These principles can be applied to other activities where there is a significant change in the environment.

2. Sensory overload. We now consider the different sensory inputs that may have an impact on some of these children. For instance, smells, such as food in a busy dinner hall, can be very overwhelming because of the way some children's brains process this information. An example is a young boy who was pre-verbal, sitting directly next to where the school dinner food is served. At the start of the term, this child refused to eat his school lunch and, with his communication difficulties, it proved hard for him to express why it was an issue. This child was moved to a different

part of the dinner hall where he was further away from where the food was served and he began to eat his lunch. This could lead us to believe that he found the smells coming from the food a sensory overload. The same difficulties can also be associated with other sensory inputs. For instance, a child who struggles in a music lesson may be sensitive to noise, and therefore a simple strategy would be to provide ear defenders. The key is to evaluate and identify the different sensory inputs when an environment changes or when a child displays distress.

3. Regulating temperature. Some children with autism may self-regulate temperatures at a different level. For example, it could be freezing outside and a child may insist they don't need a coat. The key is about educating the child at whatever level suits them – for instance, explaining that although they may not be feeling cold, their body demonstrates this in different ways, for example, goosebumps, shivering and seeing their breath. This is a better visual representation for them to understand.

4. Understanding emotions. This can be a real challenge for some children with autism. The starting point is to work on a one-to-one level

to see if that child can understand their own emotions. Strategies such as zones of regulation can be very useful, as long as there is some prior explanation about how this system works. Another strategy is that when a particular child is feeling happy, you may take a picture of that moment and at a different moment show that child the picture and see if they can explain how they felt. While we wouldn't recommend taking a picture of a child who was upset and angry, you may take a picture of the event or object that caused the distress and, when that child is in a better state, ask that child to reflect on how they were feeling. When working on emotions, perseverance is needed, since this is a very delicate subject to work on and can take a long time for progress to be seen.

5. Language. I have already referred to the Blank's Levels system a number of times, and we really must consider how our children interpret the information given, as this has a big impact on their social interactions. If children don't have the tools to communicate, school life can become very difficult.

Strategies for the classroom
There are other elements that the children we've worked with would like people to understand. The

first is eye contact. Some children with autism can struggle to make direct eye contact. The worst thing we can do is to force children into that way of communicating. As trust builds over time, children may naturally start making eye contact; however, forcing it can make it into a bigger issue. We still need to ensure we have children's attention and that they're listening by perhaps asking them to repeat back what has been said or other techniques to check attention if this is not appropriate.

Work needs to be done to prepare children for change or new situations. This is where visual timetables are important to demonstrate a change in routine. We also need to think about the amount of time we give children to process that change. For some, it could be just minutes, but for others this may need weeks of work. When visiting a new environment, we may need to make some visual pictures, a social story or a pre-visit to ensure the child feels comfortable with the new situation. We have discussed the different ways children process sensory inputs, and another to consider is taste and textures. Some children with autism may have limited diets and they only trust the food they have become familiar with, that is, the same brand. Just like with eye contact, we don't want to enforce a range of foods on young people; however, we may consider involving health professionals who can give more specialised advice around expanding their food choices. It is important to remind ourselves that sensory sensitivity could involve any of the human senses.

At this point, I would like us to reflect upon two key questions.
First: how easy is it for children in your classroom to communicate? Then consider some of the barriers we have spoken about and how you may adapt your approach to include these children. Second: what other factors may be impacting the young people with autism? You can reflect on the socialising elements we have spoken about and the different environmental factors. It is important we keep a note of what works, because, as these children travel through their education, best practice would be to build on what has worked well.

"To me it feels like a superpower, almost like I have some extra brain power."

Sensory needs
Within this section we have touched on the importance of understanding how different children

react to different sensory inputs and how this can play a big part not just in their educational experience but also in their experience of life. Meeting the needs of children is something we cover in detail during our mental health section, but it is important to also consider how specific sensory needs can have an impact on children with autism.

As professionals working in schools, it goes back to knowing the children you work with well and observing their responses in different situations (as we explained during our socialising section). Children can demonstrate their need for some level of sensory support in lots of different ways, but this could look like feet tapping, chair rocking, leaning into friends, fidgeting, going quiet, becoming overwhelmed, etc. As we mention throughout the book, it is all about knowing the individual.

To develop this section, we have worked with a school setting that has given some practical examples about how to design classrooms to support sensory needs. For example, we could start by looking at the correct seating for an individual. Traditional classroom seating may result in some children becoming slumped and switching off from the activity in hand, but a simple solution could be to use a wobble cushion or a ball. With any piece of equipment, it is always good to have clear boundaries about how it is used and explain why an individual might be using it.

A small trampoline in the classroom or within a specific sensory room may be another strategy used for some children who may need a vestibular sensory input. Other strategies for tactile needs may include vibration, messy play, tickling or light touch. A visual input may include bright lights, toys with flashing lights or bright colours to focus on.

We could also use different strategies including different smells, music, cold drinks or crunchy food. We all experience different inputs every day which some of us won't even think about. When teaching children with autism, this experience can feel very different and some may become overwhelmed. We always encourage schools to look at the big picture and see these strategies as reasonable adjustments so that children can access their education.

Role models
We know many children look up to those around

them and we want to continue looking at autism as a positive rather than a negative. There are many examples of people in past and present society who have had a diagnosis of autism. In our school sessions, we use examples such as Greta Thunberg, Chris Packham, Anne Hegerty and the creator of Pokémon, Satoshi Tajiri. There are also brilliant people from the past, such as Albert Einstein, who delivered one of the best ever quotes: "If you judge a fish by its ability to climb a tree, you will spend your whole life believing that it's stupid." I also like to add to this: "If you judge a fish by what it does in the water, you will have a very different viewpoint." Society should remember this when we consider people with autism – let's look at their strengths first. It is also important to say that a role model doesn't have to be someone famous because some people won't connect with them and they can be more relatable if it is somebody known personally.

In summary, it's all about how we scaffold children's learning. We know there are certain steps when teaching a child, a new strategy or concept, and this will start to build connections in the brain. When scaffolding for children with autism, we need to try and see things from their perspective. Autism as context blindness can make the world confusing and unpredictable, which is why our strategies may need to be adapted or repeated until the context is understood.

Addressing misconceptions
A big part of our jobs in schools is to address stereotypes. We need to create an ethos where people's differences are not only understood but celebrated. This should just naturally be a part of our curriculum. Young people have told us they have heard or have been asked about the following stereotypes:

> 1. Can I catch autism?
> We know that we can't. If you sit next to someone with autism and they sneeze, you are not going to catch it!

> 2. People with autism can't speak.
> We have already looked at different ways of communicating. There are some children with autism who may not use words but develop other strategies, whereas some children with autism can use lots of language.

> 3. People with autism don't have any

friends.

We know this is not true, but there are a few things here to consider. First, the child in the playground who is happy in their own space may look like a problem to an adult; however, this may be the space they need to desensitise from a busy classroom environment. We should never be forcing friendships upon young people, but instead making sure we are inclusive by giving them the option. At the other end of the spectrum are some children who may describe everyone as their friends because, for example, they may see the receptionist every morning. A simple technique is to ask children to write down the names of close family members and best friends in the middle of a piece of paper and then place a circle around them and build outwards from there. This can help to demonstrate levels of relationship.

4. Will children with autism have three heads?

This points to a lack of understanding. Some children who come to visit a special school setting have been scared to enter because they have an image of what autism looks like.

5. You don't look like you have autism.
My reply to this is: "What does autism look like?" Autism has no 'look'.

6. All children with autism make loud noises or stim.
Loud noises could be the child's way of communicating. In a supermarket, this could be a child's way of explaining to their parent or carer that they need the toilet. Stimming (repetitive self-stimulating behaviour) is another form of communication; for example, a child could be very happy, but rather than verbalise this, their eyes roll slightly and their hands flap. This is a form of expression. There are many ways that children can stim or express themselves and you may refer to our earlier section about getting to know an individual. This is an area in which society needs more education as social media can often belittle those who stim and it is currently seen as not socially acceptable. People express their emotions in all different ways and a lot of work needs to be done so that more people understand this.

7. Girls can't have autism.
This will be addressed in later sections, but girls can have autism.

8. Injections/vaccinations give you autism.
Scientific evidence over time has shown this to be false.

9. Everybody has a bit of autism.
This idea causes much debate, but I am basing my response on those I have worked with who have autism. It is true that we are all different and all of our brains work in various ways; however, not everyone is autistic, because that is a specific term and a diagnosed neurological condition.

Independence

Ultimately, many children with autism are going to enter a society on leaving school that can be very rigid. To ensure children have the best chances in life, we must also develop their levels of independence. Our starting point is to look at how independent they are right now. A temptation in schools, especially if a child has a one-to-one or extra support, is to feel like we need to do everything for them. Remember that many of these children can learn based on continuous routines, and if we can develop their learning of independence skills this can help them in later life. On the other hand, we should also respect the amount of support they need so that when they don't understand a process or strategy, we are willing to spend more time with them or teach in a different way. Finally, ensuring children have ambitions is very important. Many children can become disheartened because they feel different, but we must echo that difference is a good thing. Their ambitions should come from within and not from our expectations of the young person.

Masking
Masking is when a child portrays himself or herself in one way in certain environments and differently in others. In a school environment, an individual could seem as if they are handling things very well, making progress and even socialising, but when they get home this all unravels. Think of a fizzy bottle exploding after being shaken for several minutes. This is not dissimilar to what happens to some children when they have been masking all day at school. When masking becomes too much, there are negative impacts on their mental health. The pressure of masking often comes from wanting to fit in or not being

seen as different, so our first point of advice here, as always, is to create an open ethos in your classrooms by discussing our differences, the ways we cope with things and our different learning styles.

Some parents struggle when trying to make their schools believe them about their children with autism. As professionals, we must respect the fact that parents know their children best in terms of masking behaviour. If this scenario becomes apparent, first look at changes we could make to the end of the school day; for example, a small sensory break, a discussion with another adult or even a positive diary. These strategies can help release some of the behaviours that have been masked all day, but also act as a strategy to support the transition from school to home. The end of the day is not always the appropriate time for every child, so you could implement one of these strategies in the middle of the day or even in the morning, depending on the individual. Remember that the idea of masking can also occur the other way around, so an intervention may be needed when a child comes directly into school to help with any challenges.

When trying to identify if a child is masking, we

must look at their education as a whole. Ask yourself whether the child has become withdrawn from asking for support or has started to struggle in some specific areas of learning. Has the child become more anxious about trying new activities or do they have gaps in their ability to socialise and make friends? We must also look at their mental wellbeing overall, to see how they are coping in different situations.

Another example given to us about masking has been about being in pain and not having the words to explain this, or just trying to ignore it in the hope that the pain goes away. This is not simply physical pain, but also emotional pain that could be causing distress and over time could lead to more significant mental health problems. There is a real need to address difficulties early and create a suitable environment where children feel they can truly be themselves. At times, we are fighting many different battles (something we explore further in our mental health section) but those battles don't feel as large when we have people around us who can understand us. Sometimes a little understanding goes a long way, even if we as teachers don't see the effect ourselves.

ADHD awareness – Part one

<u>Understanding ADHD</u>

ADHD is real.

We make this statement straight away because ADHD is often seen as a behavioural difficulty. Every behaviour is a form of communication and it is no different for a child who has this diagnosis. We must look past the secondary behaviours and observe the root cause. Some children with ADHD can appear disruptive or defiant, but we can't just label this behaviour 'typical ADHD behaviour'. Secondly, ADHD cannot be an excuse used by children for poor behaviour, and we will discuss some positive strategies within this chapter.

Let's start by considering what ADHD stands for: Attention Deficit **Hyperactivity** Disorder. Hyperactivity is in bold because if we were to take that word away, we would be left with ADD, which is a different diagnosis. However, our focus is on the symptoms, such as inattentiveness and impulsiveness, that are linked to the diagnosis of ADHD (you can have a diagnosis of both).

Test your knowledge of ADHD:
1) Can ADHD improve with age?
2) What percentage of children with ADHD also have other associated learning difficulties?

3) What percentage of children with ADHD may also have Oppositional Defiance Disorder (ODD)?

In answer to Question 1, ADHD does not disappear with age. The window of opportunity when children are developing is crucial to ensure that, when these children get to adulthood, they have the strategies to deal with their challenging symptoms. If these strategies are in place correctly, then we see an increase in children's ability to access general society, deal with difficult situations and step outside their comfort zones. This learning is linked back to the connections that we all make every day within our brains. The ADHD brain is no different. It can be moulded, and children can start to self-regulate. The childhood period is key to ensuring that improvement can be seen with age. Many adults who had those positive experiences when they were young talk about being able to use ADHD as a positive.

I always get a varied response to Question 2 in schools, with the majority going for 60 per cent or more. Based on our research, the figure is actually around 50 per cent, so half of the children who have a diagnosis of ADHD also have other associated learning difficulties such as autism or dyslexia. Our advice is to keep an open mind when working with a child who has ADHD, because there could be other factors at play that cause that child to struggle in a certain situation, separate from the ADHD diagnosis. For example, a student may get to every English lesson happy and content, but as soon as a reading task is put in front of them, they start to struggle. The temptation can be to blame this on a lack of concentration or a busy mind, but the child could be dyslexic or have other challenges with their English skills. We must look at the whole picture and try to identify specific needs based on paying close attention to that individual. Additionally, some children can go undiagnosed with a range of learning differences, so the percentage could be slightly higher.

For Question 3 we focus on any other learning difficulties and how many of them could be made up of ODD. It is roughly 60 per cent. Whilst a lot of research is looking into the different connections between ADHD and ODD, there is still a lot more to be understood. A basic overview of ODD is that many of the behaviours link to challenges in following authority, responding to structure, not dealing with setbacks well and finding it hard to follow another person's agenda. At times, there can be a crossover between the challenges associated with both ADHD and ODD.

"We need to talk about ADHD so people understand us"

Common challenges associated with ADHD
To start to build an understanding of ADHD, these are some common challenges associated with the diagnosis. This is not a definitive list, however, because each child with ADHD is an individual.

•

- • Self-esteem. Some children with ADHD experience very low levels of self-worth, which can sometimes seem surprising because on the outside they can be louder or slightly extrovert, when inside they are masking a lot. The key is to find what makes that individual feel good about themselves, whilst reducing the need for them to compare themselves with their peers. We will return to self-esteem in more detail later.

- • Memory skills. These can be a challenge for some children with ADHD. It helps to not overwhelm the child, so when asking a question, consider the number of steps it involves. A child once explained to me that the ADHD brain can just feel "busy and fuzzy all of the time", which is why the amount of information given must be considered.

- • Making predictions. This is a challenge associated with autism, however it can be a challenge within ADHD, too. Teachers need to use preparation and give the child enough information so that they feel ready for the next lesson, activity or event. Simply assuming a child is comfortable with the next step or change can often lead to difficulties. To help this, we need to use strategies such as visual timetables, now-and-then boards or even PECS symbols.

- • A sense of time. Some children with ADHD struggle to grasp the concept of time. Our advice is to let the children make time relatable to themselves first before anything else. For example, a child may have a particular moment in the day that means a lot to them. If they link this with a particular time, they start to learn a repetition of time and can then start to apply it to other points in their daily life. Progress with this can take time, but the more we make it relatable and the more consistency we offer, the more it will stick. You can also consider using visual timetables to support children with their sense of time.

• • Fight, flight or freeze. While everyone has these responses, an ADHD mind can act more impulsively without a stop-and-think moment first. We should never deal with the behaviour at its highest point. More often than not, the child won't be ready to listen and so the priority is to wait and keep the child safe. It is very important that we do not ignore the behaviour, but instead choose a better time to approach this. When one of the three responses has started, the child will not be in the right frame of mind to take advice or make things better. Discovering what triggers each of the responses and making sure we put interventions in place before they reach their highest point is essential. We must also keep a record of this because, as a child moves from class to class, a consistent approach is needed to support that child.

- • Organisation skills. This could look like a child not putting away their school bag, leaving equipment spread out or finding it hard to give themselves a structure or routine. A good strategy in school is to provide a peer mentor who could role-model good organisational skills for them. Alternatively, an adult could give the child some gentle reminders displayed as visuals, rather than seeing the child as messy.

- • Making choices. Some children also struggle with flexibility around making choices and the temptation can be to give the child too many options. What we should do is give two clear options that the child understands, using language such as "It's this or it's that". This lets the child feel as though they are in control of the situation, but we have decided the appropriate choices and just been a little bit more flexible in our approach. It is important to say there will be times where choices cannot be made, which will be covered later in this chapter.

- • Understanding emotions. Like children with autism, children with ADHD can also struggle to understand others' emotions. See Page 14 for the importance of children understanding their own emotions first and the strategies to support this.

- • Restlessness. This won't be a surprise to many. Restlessness could be in the school day, at home or even when the child is trying to sleep. It normally signifies that they are over- or under-stimulated, and we should focus on their sensory inputs at that particular moment. For example, a child might be quite restless when they come in from school, so this wouldn't be the appropriate time to sit and discuss their day. They may need some time bouncing on a trampoline, with a screen or listening to music. These types of activities can be replicated as sensory breaks throughout the school day. Finding what works for that individual remains key.

• • Tics. It is important to state that not every child with ADHD develops tics, nor does a child have to have ADHD to develop a tic. However, some research shows there can be a link. Tics can be the body's way of expressing different energy that is developed in the brain. It may present itself as oral sounds, bodily jerks or other involuntary movements. Importantly, tics and stimming are two different things. Unlike stimming, tics are involuntary movements. Stimming is done as a way of expressing feelings, but it is again important to mention that this is very individual and there is no one way to 'stim'. There are links to further reading at the end of this book.

"We need to train teachers directly about ADHD"

ADHD understanding in further detail
PICTURE CHALLENGE 1
Let's now think more deeply about ADHD. Imagine a light bulb and three moths circling that light bulb. Take a moment to consider what this image has to do with ADHD.

There are many different answers, but we want to look at singular focus. Some children with ADHD can become very focused on one activity, often a visual one. Difficulties can occur when we ask that child to change their focus because they are so stimulated by the current activity. If we further consider the link between gaming and ADHD, this helps us to explain this theory further. Not every child with ADHD loves to play video games; however, there is a lot of research to show that gaming can really capture the ADHD brain. My challenge to schools is to look at what can be learnt from the gaming, and some elements might be added to our lessons. Obviously, I am not suggesting that we allow children to game all day, because that would not be good for their education, progress or mental health, but there are factors that can be learnt. First, consider the visual element of video games – they are bright and attractive and they draw in the attention of the gamer. If we have a great visual starter to begin the lesson, this can capture the child's attention so that they are engaged straightaway. We may then need to think about how we use that stimulus throughout the lesson.

Also, instant gratification can be provided by a good game. If we can look at small wins and shorter tasks in our lessons, this will often result in better outcomes. The child with ADHD may still complete the same task; however, it may just be cut down into smaller chunks. Another element of gaming is that there are often different levels, which keeps things fresh and exciting, and the child can also clearly see the progress they are making, which provides instant gratification. Therefore, at each point of achievement, we should try really hard to recognise what they have done and praise the effort, rather than focus on the outcome.

The moths around the light bulb can represent how children can become very hooked on one stimulus, hence the term we used: 'singular focus'. Taking all this into account, it is important we consider transitions between different activities or periods of the day. If this does cause a challenge for some of the children you teach, refer to the strategies further on in this chapter.

PICTURE CHALLENGE 2

The next image to visualise is a young person on a bike ready to go down a hill. Pause here to reflect on the relation between this picture and ADHD.

You may have thought about children needing to express energy or being on a particular journey where they become unbalanced. None of these answers would be wrong, but we are taking a slightly different angle. Referring to 'ADHD – Living without Brakes' by Martin L. Kutscher (2009) we can begin to explain this picture:

Simply put, in ADHD the frontal lobe brakes and other executive functions are asleep on the job. You already know what happens when the frontal lobes are sleepy. Just think about how typical kids act when they are over-tired and their frontal lobes are not fully awake – at midnight all six-year-olds are cranky and can't concentrate. Consider that tired secretary who is in need of a coffee break and stops working efficiently and gets chatty. Further look at what happens when people drink alcohol. Alcohol is a central nervous system suppressant (the opposite of stimulants) and puts the frontal lobes to sleep. This results in the poor self-control, poor foresight and over-talkative behaviour of people who consume alcohol. (Kutscher, Page 31)

Imagine this child on the bike travelling down a hill. For some children, when this gets too fast or there is an obstacle in the way, they will slam on their brakes. Children with ADHD can take longer to do this. We almost need to imagine that we put paths into this hill to naturally slow the bike down.

In essence, we need to increase children's and our own awareness of ADHD. One student with ADHD spoke in detail in one of our sessions about how just someone understanding him made a huge difference.

"It can make you sad because people just think you are naughty and rude."

Feelings, sleep and food
The children who helped us design these sessions were keen for us to consider two key questions:
1. How would you be feeling if you were faced with these differences?
2. What are some of the external (outside of school) factors that you think have an

impact on children with ADHD?

For Question 1, the most common responses from adults are things such as frustration, feeling very different, feeling as if I can't make friends and the sense of not being in control. I think these are important feelings to remind ourselves of when things become difficult for a child. Dealing with a distressed child can evoke responses in our own emotions, but as adults we must remain in control of the situation. We are not failing a child if at times we need to step away and swap with another adult. In times of distress, a new face can be a positive strategy to help reduce the level of response we are receiving from that child. It is always helpful to reflect on the root cause. What evoked that response? This should always be our starting point.

For Question 2, there are many areas that can be discussed. However, the two areas we focus on are sleep and food. First, some children with ADHD can struggle to sleep. Schools should look at supporting parents to get the right medical advice to see if medication before bedtime could help.

Other strategies include coming away from a visual stimulus in a good amount of time before bed, weighted blankets, soothing pillows, calming music or some meditation to help the child receive the correct sensory inputs before and during sleep.

With food, there are two different areas to think about. The first links to medication, because some children's ADHD medication can suppress their hunger or their diet. This may mean if a child has their medication mid-morning, they will then find it difficult to eat at the standard lunchtime. Where I've seen best practice is schools that adapt the time for that child so they can eat in different intervals throughout the day rather than all at once at a set time. For some children, the medication can have the opposite effect and make them ravenous. The same advice should be followed in that we should encourage the child to eat small portions throughout the day at different intervals rather than large amounts all at once.

The second issue with food is the link between children with ADHD and over-eating, which can then result in obesity. This can be surprising to many at first, because we may have a picture of the ADHD child always being on the move. Yet the impulsive side of the brain can induce compulsive eating habits. We need to educate children about a balanced diet, but also the appropriate times for when we should be eating. Children with ADHD may also need support with deciding on when to stop eating, because the part of the brain that tells them when they are full is not always functioning as quickly. The final point to make on key factors is also about sharing good practice. If you find a strategy in school that really works to support that child, you should be looking at how to replicate this in the home. Like autism, the more structure and routine we can put in place, the better chance the child will have to understand the way things work.

Strategies for the classroom
Rewards systems.
A good rewards system is usually visual, hooks the child in and results in instant gratification. With any rewards system, we must start by knowing the individual well, so there may be a hobby or interest that we can link into the system. If the child is

constantly hitting the targets of the reward system, we can also stretch them or 'level them up'. A good system should also be separate from any negative behaviour consequences. For example, if a child decided to rip down the class display, an appropriate consequence would be for the child to repair the display in their own time. That behaviour should not impact on the rewards system, because the system is all about positive reinforcement and should be separate. The system should also be realistic. If a child struggles to sit still for long periods of time, a target to sit for 40 minutes would not be realistic. As the adult in control of the rewards system, we should also have clear boundaries. The temptation at the end of a hard school day might be to give the reward even if that child hasn't met the target. If we do this once, however, the likelihood is that the child won't forget and the whole system falls apart. We may be in charge of the system overall, but the child still needs to be included to ensure they understand the structure of the system right from the start. After reading this section, you could all go away and search rewards systems or even rewards systems for children with ADHD. You may find some good templates, but our advice would be to not make these generic, but built around individual children.

When we have a good rewards system in place, communication with the home is essential. This helps us to use the same vocabulary and structure and there is more consistency for that child at home and at school. Tough days will happen. Do not tear up the rewards system on Day One but be persistent and use repetition to help the child understand.

The final recommendation with rewards systems is to build on children's strengths. For example, if a child is a talented artist, the rewards system may include an element of art which will give ownership to that child. Rewards systems can be many different formats, such as visual charts, jars filled with objects or different progress books. There is not one suggested or preferred system that will always work, so it is important to find what works for that child.

Unsurprisingly, a crucial part of supporting

children with ADHD in schools is to break up their day. A good strategy is 'time out' cards. These are normally more effective with children in Year 5 upwards; however, each child is different. 'Time out' cards give the child ownership over when they feel they need a break from an activity or classroom environment. For example, I put this strategy in place when I taught a child who had spent 75 per cent of their time outside of the classroom the year before. I knew it would not be realistic to expect him to go from this to spending all of his time in the classroom. I allowed him time throughout the day to go and kick a football or get some fresh air when he felt this was best. Obviously, there were clear boundaries on how much they could use these cards, but the aim was all about building that child's self-regulation skills. By the end of the academic year the child didn't need to use the cards because his self-regulation skills had been built.

Similarly, the idea of giving children responsibility within the classroom or around the school can have a massive positive effect on a child's self-esteem. Consider all the different jobs that could be given to children throughout your typical school day. This engagement links to the idea of having a singular focus.

Interactive games as lesson warmups also link to the idea of a singular focus, but such games may be better served midway through the lesson or even as part of the plenary. The key to any good brain break is knowing when to do it and when to stop. If either of these are mismanaged, we run the risk of over-stimulating that child. Brain breaks should get the child into the right frame of mind to learn. If we go too far, that child can then become disengaged rather than engaged.

Medication is not specifically a brain break; however, we are going to discuss it at this point because of how some people view it. A crucial point we want to make about medication is that, as teaching professionals, we should never make the final judgement on whether a child should take ADHD medication. Always take advice from health professionals. We have heard some horror stories from parents where schools have said they can't teach a child unless they are on medication. We can give our opinion on how they are performing educationally, but simply thinking that medication will resolve a situation is not helpful. Medication can work positively or negatively for any individual and can have different effects, and obviously should be left to health professionals.

Fiddle (or fidget) toys can also be helpful when trying to aid concentration within the classroom, a school assembly or anywhere a child may need it. Depending on the age of the child, there is a range of fiddle toys, from bigger toys for younger children to more discreet cubes that can fit into a child's pocket. Even something as simple as a ball of putty can help. It doesn't always have to be a toy; some children could benefit from having a doodle pad. Fiddling supports children with ADHD to be more productive by focusing their extra energy onto an object rather than possibly looking for negative responses within the classroom.

When we look at planning our lesson activities, we should keep them short, sharp and focused. They should allow enough time for the child to understand what we want them to learn, sharp enough so they don't lose interest and focused on a key area of learning. I appreciate that when considering the brain break interventions, there are also many other children in the classroom to consider, but many of these strategies can benefit a whole classroom. After reading this book, you should not try and implement all these strategies at once because it would be impossible. It's about looking at the individual and having a small toolbox that is not too time-consuming and works for the child and the teacher.

One of the final points with brain breaks is to simply have a clear structure of what you want to do. This allows you and the child to know exactly what is expected, that is, how long it will last or when it can be used. With brain breaks, we must also try to avoid competition. If you plan to use a brain break as a whole class intervention, try to steer away from making it competitive. Remember, brain breaks are there to get a child or children into the right place to learn. We do not want to over-stimulate by adding in unneeded competition.

If you have many children in your class with ADHD or suspected ADHD, it is a good idea to continue doing your own research. There are some links at the end of this book. As mentioned earlier, over 50 per cent of children who have ADHD may also have another learning difficulty. This means we should always consider the whole child and look more specifically at areas of need. Sometimes the behaviour of a child with ADHD can be challenging, but it's important to remember it is not a personal attack. If at times we feel our response to a child is not going to be productive due to how we are feeling, a change of face can be very effective. If attacks do become, or seem, personal, look at what that child is trying to tell us about how they are feeling inside.

Getting children seated in the correct place is important in all our classrooms and even more so for those with ADHD. If, for example, we know our child really benefits from a visual stimulus, seat them close enough to the interactive whiteboard. If we have a few bigger characters within our classroom, sitting two next to each other may not be productive, so we may need to think about who they are sitting near. Alternatively, sitting at the front may cause too much of a distraction or persuade the child to think they need to offer a performance, so they may need to be seated at the back.

When we give instructions, we need to ensure our speech is clear and we are direct with what we are saying. Any grey areas could be misinterpreted or used against us later. For example, if a child asks to hang off a goal post and we try to brush if off by saying: "Not today," they may just do it tomorrow because it's a new day. However, if we were to say: "No, we don't do that," we are clear with our response. Tasks that engage and promote ownership are always going to work better, so take time to explore what that child is really interested in and ensure there are strategies in place to create a sense of worth about that child's piece of work. For example, they can use a self-checker chart that prompts some of the areas of need in a piece of writing they have helped to create with you. If they are involved in that process, they are less likely to see these comments as negative.

Visual timetables help to structure a child's day. Some children with ADHD tell us they constantly feel out of control, so giving them a visual support tool can help aid this. In addition to timetables, sand timers are a simple and effective way of managing a transition or a change in focus. Some older children can feel singled out with a sand timer in front of them, so other strategies may include a small whiteboard with three marks. Every so often an adult will come past and rub a mark off to show a countdown of time. Sometimes we must think more productively about how we give feedback – for example, some children will be okay with praise in front of the class, but others may need a quiet word afterwards. We must also consider the way we use body language, as some children may prefer a discreet thumbs-up or a tap on the shoulder. For others, a written comment in a workbook or on a reward chart may be positive, too. If we get our feedback right, this can really support a child's self-esteem.

<u>ADHD awareness – Part two</u>

What is ADHD?

We always promote talking about ADHD openly. When we go into schools, we start by asking the children what ADHD is. Don't be afraid to ask these questions. You may receive some interesting responses at first, which is why education is key.

I then show the group an array of random pictures. Before looking at the screen, I invite the children to close their eyes if they feel comfortable. As they open their eyes, I ask the group which picture they are drawn to first. This often gets a mixed response, but I make the point that after seeing one picture, many of you will start looking at the others. The difference with ADHD is that our eyes can stay focused on one singular picture. So, when a child struggles to change from one activity to the next, they are not being difficult. It is the way their brain is operating, which is why certain strategies should be put in place. I then play a clip from our podcast series 'The Multi-Schools Lowdown'. The episode ADHD showcases a young boy I have worked with over many years and he talks at the start of this episode about what ADHD means to him.

I reiterate that this is a difference in the brain and not something that makes children naughty or less able. We include a quiz in this session which has four famous people on a screen. I refer to Emma Watson, Jim Carey, will.i.am and Justin Bieber, all of whom have a diagnosis of ADHD. I talk about each person and how they have channelled their abilities into what they do now. There are many examples of famous people with ADHD, and my advice is to choose a few based on who you think will inspire your class the most. However, as mentioned in our role models section in the autism chapter, some children may not relate to famous people and thinking about people closer to them could have a more positive effect.

Misconceptions

The most common of misconceptions around ADHD include:

- ADHD can be caught.
- People with ADHD have too much energy.
- You can't ever grow out of ADHD.

- Children with ADHD must take medication.
- Children with ADHD have tics.
- People with ADHD can't get jobs.
- Children with ADHD can't make friends.

Let's break these down individually.

ADHD can be caught. I usually ask the group whether this is true, which receives a mixed response. We explain that you can't catch ADHD and, just like autism, it is something that you are born with or develops at a young age (this a highly researched area that you may want to investigate further).

People with ADHD have too much energy. I emphasise here that the word 'too much' should be taken out because it's about how we use our energy and not seeing it with a negative connotation. If the extra energy can be channelled into something else, often this can help somebody work at a greater speed or with closer detail.

You can't grow out of ADHD. We have covered this on Page 22; however, it is something that children seem to ask. I use a similar response with children as with adults by talking about the importance of finding the right strategies at an early age, because although this won't make ADHD disappear, it can reduce some of the associated challenges such as impulsive behaviour, a lack of attention or challenges with memory skills.

Children with ADHD must take medication. We have discussed medication already and children also have their own questions on the subject. Not all children with ADHD have to take medication. This is a personal choice and should be the choice of the family following health professionals' advice.

Children with ADHD have tics. We have discussed tics in the autism section and although they can be linked to some children with ADHD, not all children with ADHD have tics and you can also develop a tic without having ADHD.

People with ADHD can't get jobs. In the same lesson we already give examples of famous people with ADHD so we know that this shouldn't be a barrier to getting a job. I make the point that although education can try to put children into boxes, children don't fit into boxes and our brains all work very differently, so when looking for work we can build on our strengths.

Children with ADHD can't make friends. This

often evokes strong responses amongst the groups I speak to. Many children defend their friends who have ADHD saying: "Of course they have friends." I state that we must know the individual, so at times that child may want some space on their own, but this does not mean they don't want friends or can't play in a group. We may just need some extra strategies to help support these children.

Reflecting on ADHD

The final part of the lesson sees us discuss how we can simply be kinder to each other, no matter our differences. This is important when teaching any age group because children with differences are often more likely to be singled out or disrespected. The ethos you create in your classroom is crucial to underpinning your own understanding of children's differences.

At this point you may consider what challenges you feel you face in regard to teaching children with ADHD. I would then recommend picking out a couple of strategies from this chapter that you feel may work for the individuals in your classroom. If, after reading the autism and ADHD sections, you still have some questions, please feel free to email me on the contact details at the back of this book.

Mental Health in Schools

Our work in this area began back in 2017, when children began telling us that they needed more mental health support in schools. At the same time, the government released a green paper document with the idea of collecting views on what people felt would work to support children's mental health in schools. We spent some time meeting with over a hundred children across Essex to discuss their priorities and respond to the green paper. The key word which came out from young people at that time was resilience. This led us to create a resilience programme that was first trialled in a special needs school. The fact that we trialled it in a special needs school was important, because many approaches towards mental health support are initially aimed at children without SEND; but we wanted to ensure this programme was applicable for all needs. We are very passionate about this because some children with additional needs are left in limbo without the correct support for their mental health.

We will expand on the resilience programme further, but we start by talking about our staff mental health awareness sessions. Our opening line to schools is that good health should be the most cherished thing that any of us can have. This has been highlighted even further by the ongoing pandemic, where we have had to place health needs before anything else. It is vital that we do not just concentrate on physical health, but mental wellbeing too. Children are never in the right place to learn unless their mental health is in a good state. These sessions focus on the emotional wellbeing of children and how we can make small changes to ensure all children can feel at their best. You can look at the mental health continuum, which explains the different stages of mental wellbeing. What these sessions do not focus on are the children who have already developed high-end mental health difficulties, as these children need specialist support and provision. These sessions are designed to maintain children's mental health and act as early prevention strategies so that they don't develop greater mental health difficulties further down the line. All children and adults can be affected, but if we have strategies in place, most of this distress can be reversible. Before we start discussing strategies and ideas, I have two key questions for you to consider:

1: What do you do currently to support children's wellbeing within your classroom?

2: What does your school have in place outside of your classroom to promote positive wellbeing?

<u>Maslow's Hierarchy of Needs</u>
In our opinion, every member of staff working in a school should be aware of Maslow's Hierarchy of Needs. Like any model, there are flaws, such as a lack of diversity used when testing. However, the children we have worked with really understand the basic concepts and it links well into our thinking behind building resilience, too. The model is used in both our resilience programme and these mental health awareness sessions.

The basic concept is that every person has needs, visualised as a pyramid and split into five horizontal sections. In the bottom section of the pyramid are the basic needs that keep us alive, such as food, water and warmth. Above our basic needs are our safety needs, which obviously include everything that helps us to feel safe in different situations. On top of our safety needs are our belongingness and love needs, which include the important people around us. In the next layer up from this are our self-esteem needs, which are things that help us feel good about ourselves. Finally, at the top of our pyramid are our self-actualisation needs, which include reaching our full potential and whatever a positive self looks like to us. The idea is that the only way we can get to the top of our pyramids is if all the needs below have been met. Children's needs don't differ greatly from those of adults; however, our emotional intelligence levels are still being developed in childhood, so further strategies may need to be suggested to support young people's mental health. This chapter focuses on each area of need and looks at what can be done to support each layer.

Basic needs

When we started to roll out these sessions, I had a debate with a staff member who said the basic needs of young people were not the responsibility of a school. If we were looking at the world through rose-tinted glasses, this staff member might have had a point; however, this is not reality for lots of children and there are plenty of things we can do to support this layer. In an ideal world, basic needs such as food, warmth and other essentials that we take for granted would all be provided in the family home. However, we accept that this is not always the case due to a range of circumstances, and our education system should not simply be about the 'education' but actually ensure children have the basics they need to even start accessing their learning. At this stage it is important to remind ourselves that children will never learn unless they are in the right position to learn. Schools can support this by looking at things like breakfast clubs. Really good breakfast clubs are those which don't just provide nutrition but also encourage communication and may include music and allow a safe space for children in the morning.

Checking in with children in the morning is very important; however, it is also important at different points in the school day. When you have 30 to 40 children in a class, this can be challenging. In my own practice, I kept a list of all the children in the class and ensured that I had at least one meaningful conversation with each child once a week. If you are lucky enough to have additional staff within the classroom, this can be part of their role. It is important that each child feels valued. You may read this and feel a week is unrealistic, but we should ensure it is happening at least every two weeks. Worry boxes are another popular approach. Young people can add their worries to a slip and place it in a box which is checked by school staff. Interestingly, some children have told us they feel they are being watched if the worry box is in their classroom, so some schools now have boxes placed in different areas throughout the school. Slips don't always have to include words – they could be pictures, as this is how some children best communicate their feelings and communication needs are different for all.

The link between exercise and positive mental health is one we can't ignore. This is not to say that everybody will want to go for a run or play competitive sport; however, raising the heart rates of children, getting them outside and doing something active should be planned into our school days in some way.

As this section is looking at early intervention strategies, we should also be mindful of the fact that we can only do so much. If we feel a child is at risk of developing greater mental health difficulties, we should be aware of the support services in our area, and if children's basic needs are not being met, this is when we must act. If you are not currently aware of external services or the procedures within your own setting, then you should talk to your school's safeguarding lead or another appropriate member of staff.

An activity suggested by a local mental health service is to ensure there is a positive starter to the school day, such as having a power point presentation of furry animals as children enter the classroom. When delivering these sessions in person, often adults smile at the thought of this and smiling or positive thoughts are what we are aiming for in children with these types of activities. Depending on the age you are working with or the interests of your class, it doesn't have to be furry animals; you could have an alternative theme or subject that will promote positivity. It could also include something humorous as there is also a lot of research into the positive impact of laughter on our mental wellbeing.

As part of meeting our basic needs, we should also be building a better understanding of mental health in children so that, ultimately, they have a better understanding of themselves. This is so much more than just talking about mental health in a PSHE lesson, and instead making it part and parcel of each day. This should include an openness to talk about our feelings, the use of strategies such as zones of regulation, a variety of staff who are available to chat with and displays around school to promote positive mental health.

One of the reasons we have such a stigma around mental health is because we don't talk about it enough with young children. As staff, we must be confident in discussing mental health and empower children to do the same. Many of these points seem very basic, which is why they come under our 'basic needs'. If children's basic needs aren't being met, this should be an area for our safeguarding teams to investigate as mentioned earlier. To repeat, without a child's basic needs being met, they will struggle to make any progress. This thread continues throughout each layer as we climb up the pyramid.

Safety needs
What makes you feel safe? Take some time to consider this as we explore what we can do in schools to ensure children feel safe. On asking this question in staff training, I usually get responses such as: 'family members', 'having a routine', 'understanding what's coming next' and 'a safe place to sleep'. As we grow, our safety needs can change, yet many children still relate to a lot of these needs. Like a spider web, many of our safety needs can cross over and can be quite complex in formation. There are many aspects to safety, but we focus on a handful that we find are most common for children.

First, a lack of information can lead to feelings of uncertainty and anxiety, which is why preparation for a new activity or a change in scenery can often be needed. When working with children who have additional needs, prior information is even more important, and so we would use tools such as visual timetables and social stories. Another aspect of safety is children's understanding of a situation. This ties in with communication and language needs and having tools in place to allow children to communicate in different ways if something doesn't work for them. We discuss the importance of communication in more detail in the next section.

Food can also play a role in our safety needs as well as our basic needs. If a child does not eat enough or has an unbalanced diet, this can impact on how they feel in different situations. For example, a child who has not eaten breakfast – or even possibly dinner the night before –– may well be very unsettled when they start the school day, and a morning intervention may be needed.

Attachment issues can play a big role in how safe a child feels. In this book we will not go into much detail of attachment as this is a very complex issue; but if you are interested to find out more you could investigate how to become an **attachment aware school.**

Some children talk to us about the difficulty they face when arriving at school. Equally, schools can face problems when trying to encourage children in through the school gates. One strategy we have seen work well is when a safety object is given to the child via the parents, and they take it with them into the school so that they feel comfortable that this object will be passed back to the parent as they return home. For some children, more work may be needed, and we would recommend something along the lines of a social story that explains the process of going to school. A good social story might include a picture of the child and reference pictures that are part of their process when arriving at school. For example, a picture of the school, potentially a staff member meeting them, and then where they go next. In our autism section, we discussed how some children can struggle to visualise a new situation, which is why resources like this can make a big difference. The next safety need is temperature. In our classrooms we should consider the temperature, because if a child is too cold or hot this can impact on how safe they feel. Whilst writing this book we are still in Covid times where many classrooms have to be better ventilated, which affects the classroom temperature. We should consider this and possibly adapt the amount of movement breaks we have within the school day.

Bullying can obviously affect how safe a child feels. Unfortunately, we are aware of many issues faced by all children, but especially those with additional needs. We should create an ethos in our classrooms and our schools that accepts all our differences because, if we don't, the consequences are serious both in and out of school. With the advancement of technology and the rise in popularity of social media, bullying issues have become more apparent. We should always look at early intervention strategies when it comes to bullying incidents. A comment that can be described as just 'banter' one day can quickly develop into a more serious issue. The quicker we respond and clamp down on these issues, the better chance we have of preventing more severe bullying incidents. Part of this work is also about addressing the stigma of somebody being a 'grass' and we need to encourage children to report bullying incidents. Many schools now have children who act as anti-bullying ambassadors, which is a very good way to promote responsibility and ensure children are keeping each other safe.

A big part of our role in the classroom is

understanding the social dynamics. This is as important as promoting their academic targets. We should consider children's seating arrangements and how they may be influenced by certain peers. Children may not always be forthcoming about their seating needs or even understand the need for being seated in the correct place. Therefore, we must be good observers in our role as classroom staff. Some children may try and struggle through the day, which can have an adverse effect on their mental health over time.

Another area to consider is a lack of sleep. First, think about your own reactions when you haven't had a good night's sleep as an adult and how these differ from days when you have. As adults, we have developed some self-regulation skills, whereas children are still very much working on these. When the brain is tired, our fight, flight and freeze responses may be triggered differently, which results in different behaviour. We need to be keeping a track of behaviour that is out of character when situations become tougher to see if there is a pattern with things like lack of sleep. Our communication with the home is vital all of the time, but even more so when there may be challenges; and if we need to provide a mixed approach on those days so that things don't become overwhelming then we should. It is also important for children to understand the impact on their mental wellbeing when they don't get enough sleep.

Substance abuse plays a role in how safe children feel. We must educate children about the impact of drugs and alcohol. As with sleep, we need to keep a record of changes in behaviour. Problems such as 'county lines' have been highlighted in the press and it is always good to be aware of local programmes that may be able to address some of these problems.

The second issue here is adults using illegal substances in a child's home environment, with potentially unpredictable behaviour and consequences. This impacts how children form relationships within schools as they may become untrusting or form relationships with other children to seek comfort, even though these relationships may be unstable or inappropriate. Early interventions are needed here, and we must ensure we are recording this as part of our safeguarding responsibilities.

In this book we have already spoken about sensory inputs and how different sensory inputs can affect how safe a child feels in a certain situation – for example, the lighting in the room, the noise, any different smells, different language that's used, the feel of a material, etc. This is very individual and it's important we have a clear picture of that child and what might be needed to ensure those sensory needs are met in a school environment.

Belongingness and Love Needs
When working with children, we see the impact friendships can have on children's mental health. With the impact of Covid 19, children have also had to adapt the way they form friendships. This has been both positive and negative, but when friendships go wrong it can play a big role in how resilient children feel. When working on our resilience programme, many children told us that before they seek out an adult or a counsellor, they would rather discuss their problems with a trusted friend. This means that we need to look at how we are promoting friendships in schools and discussing the important role they play in children's development, especially when it comes to resilience.

We focus on the importance of communication and the role this plays in friendships. If a child struggles to communicate, they will often lack confidence, which will impact not just their friendships but also their engagement in the class. Additionally, they may fail to communicate with staff, so when they are unwilling to speak or don't have the skills to do so, the issues that affect their mental health, have subsequent effects on their educational progress. To ensure we boost children's communication skills, there are some simple strategies.

Communication games for different age groups are a key starting point. Games should focus on children's speaking and listening skills and not just solely on one area. In each lesson, you should allow opportunities for children to communicate with each other, even if just for a short period. Whilst in the class, we should also encourage children to work with different partners and groups so that they are experiencing a range of personalities. However, some children with additional needs may find change difficult and this is where your knowledge of everyone is key and how you adapt to this will be important. As part of developing communication in the classroom, we should also talk openly talk about our mental health as previously mentioned. Tools such as zones of regulation can come in handy for this.

These tools should be dropped in at different points of the day rather than as a one-off so that it becomes part of everything we do and talking about our feelings and emotions is not seen as a scary activity.

We have already mentioned the importance of 'check-ins'. These should form part of different lessons where children are supporting each other and discussing how they feel about certain tasks or situations. Building on this, lots of schools now use peer role models such as having mental health ambassadors around the school or in each class. This is important because children often listen to each other, more than they will adults. We make sure that if children are discussing their issues with one or two children, these children are also supported so that they don't become overwhelmed by the thoughts or feelings of their peers. Developing children's ability to listen is something already done in class, but allowing time to develop this skill is crucial, too. A simple activity we use here is pairing children up as Partner A and Partner B. The As have the opportunity to talk about themselves for 30 seconds while Bs simply listen. At the end of the 30 seconds, Bs have to relay the information they have just been told. The roles are then swapped to ensure each child gets to talk and to listen. If you wanted to add a resource into this, you could ask the children to make their own visual top trump card – for example, writing down their strengths and possibly some interesting facts about themselves. We must see communication as a cycle. If one part breaks down, it affects the whole process. Being able to communicate how we feel can become increasingly difficult as we get older if the hard work is not put in during childhood.

Self Esteem

What is self-esteem and why is it so important? We are focusing on children's self-esteem, but as adults, it is important that we understand our own, too. We start by looking at a simple activity that every classroom can try. Put the children into a group and ask one child to leave the classroom. While they are outside, write that child's name in the middle of a piece of paper and ask all the other children to list positive attributes about them. Write these attributes down, and when everyone is finished, invite the child back in. You can then share these comments with that child and see if they can guess who said what. For some children, you may need to make adaptations, such as not sharing the comments with them, or doing the activity in a much smaller group with comments given one to one. For many children we have worked with, this activity works well because they really respond positively to the feedback from their peers rather than feedback always coming from an adult. For those who feel comfortable, I keep these pieces of paper on display in the class so that when things get tough, we can refer to the positive attributes listed. Going hand in hand with this activity is the idea of making children aware of the power of their words. It's important for children to recognise the positive or negative affect they can have on somebody else's self-esteem just with the words they use. We believe phrases such as 'sticks and stones may break my bones, but words will never hurt me' are completely outdated and should not be a culture we strive to create. The culture we would like to see is one where communicating our positive feelings towards one another becomes the norm and children support each other without needing the structure of an activity in the first place.

There are many more strategies we can put in place starting with positive praise. We can reflect on our own practice to note how often we use positive language compared with negative. Research shows that it is much easier to use negative language rather than focus on positivity.

We should ensure that our classroom practice promotes positivity, and refrain from using too much language that holds negative connotations. When you are giving praise to individuals, you must work out how they best receive that praise. For some, a comment in front of the class is okay. Others may need a comment to be made in private or even on a small note in their exercise book.

Getting children to focus on their own individual targets is also important for their self-esteem. We know that children can feel under pressure to compare themselves with others, especially within school. Giving children the opportunity to focus on their own targets allows them to concentrate on themselves. These targets should not be academic but more about their personal qualities. They could be the small steps they are taking in life, for example, becoming more helpful, swimming another length or cleaning up their equipment. The important thing is that they should be realistic and personal.

Regular check-ins are something we continue to mention as this also plays a role in how children feel about themselves. Consider how often you have spoken to each child in your class over the past two weeks. There is nothing wrong in changing the time allocated to a specific lesson and spending time just to build relationships with children. The more confident you are in this, the better place the children will be in.

We all like rewards from time to time, and when we are working towards a goal, they not only motivate us but also boost our feelings of self-esteem. In the classroom, we should consider how we reward children for positive actions based on targets they have set and also when they achieve academic milestones. Giving children the chance to reflect on what makes them an individual is important. We can do this in structured reflection times when children get into circles and discuss their positive thoughts about the week or what they are proud of. The more we repeat activities like these, the more they start to become the norm. Although self-esteem is about promoting individual strengths, you could also get the children to reflect on each other and get them to highlight the progress of their peers.

Confidence-building is another area that links to self-esteem. We can reflect on our own classroom practice and consider how many opportunities we give the children to boost their confidence.

For example, can they lead part of a lesson? Can they present in assemblies? Give ownership to young people. We can also discuss children's safety zones. Children draw out a circle and inside that circle they list the places, objects and times which help them feel most safe. Around this circle, the children can put down areas where they feel unsafe or things that are outside their comfort zone. At different stages children can reflect on these and we can then get them to think about how and when they step out of their comfort zone to help build their confidence. Some of these suggestions can fit well into a PSHE curriculum; however, if we are serious about improving children's mental health, these types of strategies need to be delivered more than once a week. For example, writing activities such as these can be combined with handwriting practice so as to focus on both wellbeing and more traditionally 'everyday' activities. It does not need to be a stand-alone activity.

As adults, we can also play a key role in supporting children's self-esteem by remembering what children tell us. A head teacher's account of an experience he had with a child is a good example. During a lunchtime conversation, the head teacher told a child about some new trainers he had bought for a long walk. The child was really interested and two years later, during another conversation, the same child asked the head teacher: "How did you get on with those trainers, sir?" I discussed this with the head, who said he felt very appreciated by that young person in taking the time to listen and remember what he had told him. We have the opportunity in our classrooms to have meaningful conversations with the children we work with. Remembering facts or stories about what they have told us can play a huge role in making them feel appreciated, rather than just a number on the school roll. Acknowledging a child as they come into the class or when they leave to go home sounds simple, but we can sometimes forget it. Making sure we take time to do this is important for children's self-esteem because it shows we care and the child feels recognised. Acknowledging them at different points throughout the day and noticing the small things is as important as when they hit a big classroom target. This may all sound very simple, but it's easy to forget when we are worrying about lesson planning or an Ofsted inspection. Nothing should be more important than children's wellbeing.

If we can get these layers right, then children have

a much better chance of reaching the top layer named self-actualisation.

Moving On

In this section, we look at transitions and the impact they can have on children's wellbeing. We know from speaking to many children that change and moving on can often be a challenge and we want to consider some strategies that may help. One of the biggest mistakes we can make is not to talk about change or transition and just brush the subject under the carpet. Often, if a child is asking us about a change that is coming up, that is because they want to talk about it and we should find time to answer questions or reassure them. We should always try and provide as much information as possible and consider the way we give this information in line with what works for them. Some children will benefit from more visual information – for example, a picture of the setting they may be visiting. Some children may need things written down or displayed using symbols. Transitions also include moving from year group to year group and, as well as building relationships with new staff, it is important to discuss any changes to the structure of the day; how workloads may change; and how expectations may be slightly different. During times of change, children often lean on those who are closest to them, so it is important for us to know who these people are and understand them. Problems can be referred onto those people so that the child feels supported. When many of us think about change, we often consider the negatives before the positives. When working with children, we should try to switch the focus to the positive elements of the transition and use a growth mindset. If possible, visits to new environments are always recommended. During the pandemic this has been difficult, but many schools have adapted by using virtual online tours or setting up zoom calls with appropriate staff.

Communication with new placements is essential to safeguard the children we work with. It is particularly important if we have a child who has experienced mental health challenges to ensure that any support they may have received is continued where necessary. It is the responsibility of both the new placement and the old placement to put the paperwork in place. A failure to pass on any documentation or relevant information can result in dramatic consequences, so it is of utmost importance. Many children tell us that inappropriately supported transitions increase their anxiety, make building friendships harder, give them a fear of failure and can lead them to feeling excluded from the new environment.

Covid 19

It goes without saying that the pandemic has had an impact on everybody, and children are not immune to this. Each child has their own personal experiences of the effects of Covid 19, but we want to collect the common points that young people have told us about. We have spoken to children from different backgrounds at various points during the pandemic and the biggest challenge was the lack of social interaction with their friends. While some children may have been fortunate enough to use technology to meet digitally, it is not the same as meeting friends face-to-face; and, of course, not all children had the means for digital communication. On returning to school, one of the big areas of concern from school staff was around speech, language and communication skills. For some children, technology has aided communication, but this has not been the case for others, and in fact has potentially impeded their development. To help support this, you could reflect on our earlier section where we discussed the belongingness and love needs for children. All children learn in different ways and we should explore how we can use technology creatively to build on some of the positive ways that young people have learnt to communicate during this time.

Children are keen for us to emphasise that everybody has had their own experiences of the pandemic. For some children, spending a lot of time within a safe home environment would have helped to ease anxieties and could have resulted in some educational benefits. When children are transitioning back to school, we must look at what has been working for that child and whether there is anything we can do to replicate the way they have been learning. We must also consider different family situations where there could be heightened anxiety amongst parents and carers and the impact this can also have on children. For others, the return to school could be a real positive, and we must build on and capture such enthusiasm. We also know that a lot of children have not had the opportunity to get outside very much during different points of the pandemic. We can look creatively at promoting outdoor learning in our school settings. Initiatives such as Forest Schools and The Daily Mile are popular and provide a break from being stuck between four walls. There is also a long list of health benefits to both our physical and mental wellbeing by getting outdoors.

Just like with transitions, one of the worst things we could do is to dismiss Covid 19 as if it has simply disappeared. It is important that we strike the right balance between bringing up the subject and moving on. If children have questions, we should find the time to answer them appropriately. Simply brushing concerns under the carpet can cause anxiety to build. We must also be aware of the media influences around children and some of the rhetoric they may hear. For example, the phrase 'catch up' was used by news outlets when children were returning to school, adding pressure to the expectations upon them. Reassuring children that we don't need to remain focused on phrases like these is important. Although children may not listen or watch the news directly, they may pick up these messages subconsciously through parents or other social media channels.

One of the big changes in schools was the move to bubbles or contained groups. For many, this resulted in smaller numbers in the playground during break and lunchtimes and for some children this was a real positive. We know from working with some schools that they have kept this structure in place to allow some children the opportunity to interact in smaller groups, which they find less daunting. This is something you could look to implement at your own school. Speak to the children and discuss other things that may have worked more positively for them during a challenging time. We must also take time to rebuild any learning opportunities that have been missed and not expect every child to come back at the same level. Our reflection-based strategies can really support both children and adults to find a common ground on where that child is at. As mentioned, it is about finding a balance and ensuring we do not put untold pressure on children. I have often heard school staff described as being 'dealers in hope', which means even when situations are difficult for us, we need to try and build positivity in the classrooms and schools.

The final topic of discussion to come out from speaking to children during the pandemic has been the importance of subjects such as art and music in their education. Many children spoke about the positive effects that drawing on a notepad or putting on some headphones had on their overall wellbeing. We should consider how we utilise these subjects during the different parts of the school curriculum or use them as interventions through the week because they can be so beneficial.

Social Media

The world of social media has been growing
for years and we are seeing its direct impact
on children and schools. Some schools that we
have worked with now have a member of their
safeguarding team focusing solely on children's
use of social media. This enables school staff
to stay up-to-date with developments on social
media and pinpoint any common problems with
certain platforms. When we deliver mental health
awareness sessions in schools, we show school
staff different logos of social media platforms to
see how many of them they recognise. The reason
we do this is to make staff aware of what children
might be using, so if any common words or
applications are discussed, staff understand them
and are able to deal with any potential issues.

We recommend doing this with your staff team
every six months as the applications that children
use are constantly evolving. This makes your
safeguarding policy more secure and means you
are aware of any problems social media may
be causing for different peer groups within your
school. There are external companies which work
with schools around the safe use of social media,

and we recommend exploring your local area to see what companies are available to deliver this e-safety training as it is an essential part of keeping children safe.

There are also positive uses of technology in regard to children's mental health. Children are going to access technology regardless of whether we agree with it or not, and as school staff we should try to embrace it positively. The idea of mindfulness is something that is commonplace across some schools and there are many apps that promote this. MindShift, Positive Penguins and SAM are three that are recommended by Mental Health First Aid England and which we would recommend starting with. Remember that applications change all the time and it is always good practice to regularly have a look at what is out there. Many children have spoken to us about the positive impact meditation or listening to music can have at different parts of the day. Therefore, we should explore opportunities where children can learn to take on these strategies independently.

Family
As school staff, part of our role is to work effectively with parents and carers. The more

effective our relationships, the better impact on children's mental health. As a school, you should consider how you build relationships with parents – for example, coffee mornings, pieces of work displayed, or updates on what's happening in the school day – so that family members feel connected to children's educational journey. As best we can, we should try and understand the family dynamics for each individual and any sudden changes can then be considered. We all – subconsciously or consciously – live by our own certain standards, but it is important we don't compare those with others when looking at how individuals may choose to live their lives. The most important place to start when considering the children we teach is Maslow's Hierarchy of Needs. Are their basic needs being met? Then we can look further up the hierarchy and think about the other needs which will be important for children's growth and development. Just like the strategies we have spoken about for helping children to communicate, we must also have strategies for parents and carers. It is important that all our communication with parents and carers remains professional and the child's wellbeing is always at the centre of our discussions. We must also consider that if a child is struggling with their own mental health, this can have an impact on the rest of the family and we should be aware of local services that may be able to offer support for the whole family.

We have discussed early intervention strategies, not severe mental health challenges or strategies for those who are already receiving high-level mental health support. If you have concerns about a child's mental wellbeing, the earlier you look to act, the better. There are some links to useful mental health charities at the end of the book, all of whom may be able to give more detailed support and advice.

Resilience building

Part of our early work with children on mental health awareness included the idea of developing children's resilience. This is something we have built upon over the years and we have created our own resilience programme. The starting point was to look at what children felt affected their resilience positively or negatively and to design a programme that addressed some of these needs. In preparing to deliver this programme, we trialled the content within a local special needs school to see how the children responded to the activities and strategies we had planned. The reason for starting within a special school was based on the young people's thoughts around how children with special needs are always an afterthought and how programmes are often adapted for them rather than starting with their needs first. We received some positive feedback which then helped us to plan a roll-out within our local area where both mainstream and special schools could benefit from a resilience programme. Whilst writing this book, we are also in the process of writing a full manual that details how to teach the resilience programme to your children which we will refer to later. However, here we are going to pick out some of the key strategies that could support not only children's resilience but also their overall mental wellbeing.

A good place to start would be to ask the children what resilience is, what it means to them and how they could become more resilient. One of the myths of resilience is that resilient people are super-strong and nothing affects them. We should correct this idea early on and talk about how showing emotions is not a sign of weakness, nor does it make you any less resilient.

Emotions and Worries

To build on our thinking around sharing emotions, you could start by asking children what worries them. Some common themes that have come up from the children we have worked with have been:

- Struggling in school
- Making mistakes
- Money
- Losing a friend
- People or animals passing away.

Once you have discussed general worries, you can then introduce the bucket strategy. Give the children a piece of paper and ask them to draw a bucket. Inside the bucket, the children should add any worries they may have. Next, give the children a highlighter or a coloured pen and ask them to highlight or underline the worries that they feel they can control. Those worries which they feel they can't control are left blank. After a few moments, ask the group if any of them would like to share any worry they feel they can control and talk about making a small change or seeking help to address it. For example, a worry that comes up is not achieving a target in a lesson. The child may feel they can control this issue by simply trying their best or seeking help if they don't understand. This forms part of a logical response to a problem.

A common example of a worry children feel they can't control is their parents getting ill or divorced.

What we discuss in regard to this is your choice to live in the moment and make the most of what you have around you rather than focusing on what happens next or what could go wrong. We accept that these worries are totally rational, but we want to reduce the effect they have on us by finding ways to cope with them. The important message with the bucket is that it's okay to worry but it's not okay to let those worries overflow, like a bucket filled with water. We then refer to our brains and liken them to a bucket being filled, which is why we must find outlets so that we don't become overwhelmed. To support this activity, you could use some buckets and get the children filling them with water to demonstrate this in person. You can finish the drawing by getting the children to add a tap to their buckets. Once they've identified the worries they feel they can control, these worries can start to flow out of the tap. The worries that are left inside the bucket will need managing through different outlets which we will explore later in this section. When completing any of these activities, it is important we remain consistent with our language so that the children understand these strategies over time.

Children's needs

Maslow's Hierarchy of Needs is something we have spoken about in detail already. For the model to work effectively, we need to start educating children about meeting their own needs. You can share the Maslow model with children and explain what each section means before asking them to design their own pyramid. Let them focus on each section and add in anything they believe supports their needs. For example, the bottom layer can include the amount of sleep they think they need, what foods they feel they should be eating, how they keep warm, etc. Above this layer are their safety needs, so ask them what helps them to feel safe. The third layer includes the important people around them and those who help them to feel as if they belong. Above this, put the child's self-esteem needs, which normally need a lot more input from the adult leading the session but ultimately consist of what helps that child to feel good about themselves. Their top layer is what 'good' looks like to them. This is when they feel their best, do their best and are their best. Spend some time on this and keep in mind the language you use.

The next part of this strategy is to have the children draw a ladder next to their pyramid. Ask the group if it is realistic to be at the top of the pyramid every single day. None of us can always be at the top, which is why the ladder comes in handy. For example, one morning you may be up the ladder in the self-esteem layer, but when you get to school somebody says something to you that's unkind and hurtful. You must then climb down the ladder and check your needs in the belongingness and love needs layer, which may include seeking out a familiar member of staff or a good friend. If a staff member or friend is not available, you may need to climb down that ladder again and check your safety needs. This could result in finding a safe place, or spending time with someone you trust, which is the same as other layers and it's why you can start to see how these overlap with each other. If no such place or person is available, you must continue to climb down the ladder until you reach your basic needs. This could mean simply taking a rest, grabbing some food or having a drink and we call this the **reset section**.

Once you have reset, you can then start to climb back up that ladder and feel as if you are in a better place to be yourself and learn. We must reiterate that nobody is going to be at the top of their game every day. In terms of the hierarchy of needs, this is because it's not possible for all our needs to be met every single day. The ladder is important because it reminds us of the simple things that can make a big difference and result in us becoming more resilient to everyday problems. A good idea would be to have a picture of this strategy in class as a reminder.

Uniqueness

When building resilience in young people, another strategy is focusing in on what makes them unique. This book has a focus on children with SEN. Often, many of these children can feel marginalised and different from their peers, which can have a negative effect on their mental health. Part of building resilience is being comfortable in your own skin. For a child who has been diagnosed with, for example, autism or ADHD, part of understanding themselves is also understanding their diagnosis. A child with ADHD may feel as if they have lots of energy, which could be seen as a negative in a school environment; however, we can point out how many tasks they may be able to achieve in a shorter period of time. A child who has autism may struggle in some social situations but will have strengths in certain subjects and find solutions that others cannot. These are generalisations, of course. Resilience building really must be individual, but the key is to focus on our strengths and what can make us more resilient. We know that children's self-esteem plays a massive role in how resilient they become. A saying that we like to use is: "You were born an original, don't die a copy."

Finding an outlet

Just as with 'resilience', we should start by asking children what they believe an 'outlet' means in relation to their wellbeing. Before getting them to list their outlets, we can demonstrate some examples in the class. For example, playing a couple of minutes of soothing music while the children close their eyes or simply sit still is easy to implement. There are also plenty of online videos to support simple yoga exercises. You may also get the children outside to take part in the daily mile. Or you could give them a piece of paper and ask them to draw or write how they feel. We hope the education system is becoming more in touch with children's needs, and we provide some useful links at the end of this book for activities that could link to children's outlets.

Another strategy to explore outlets further is to ask children to draw a picture of a dinner plate. Then ask the children to divide this plate into a few different sections. Within each section, ask the children to list different outlets which they feel make a positive difference to their wellbeing. For example, one section may list different activities they enjoy. This could be things like playing football, listening to music or playing a computer game. Another section may list the things they enjoy eating, whilst another could include people or animals, they enjoy spending time with. You may notice some crossover between this strategy and Maslow's Hierarchy of Needs, but we call this model our wellbeing plates. The thinking behind our wellbeing plates is that, historically, schools have promoted initiatives such as five-a-day and healthy eating without always considering everything else that plays a part in our wellbeing. Getting children to use a wellbeing plate encourages them to think about the right balance of different outlets they should have in their lives. For example, playing a computer game can be a positive outlet for a young person; however, spending hours playing without taking a break or eating has a negative impact on other areas of their wellbeing plate. That is why balance is very important for children to understand. Once the basics of the plate have been created, you could always turn this into an extended art activity using actual paper plates or transfer it into a computing lesson where they create their own plates using technology.

The wellbeing plate should be something to refer to as part of a child's toolbox when supporting their mental health. Without positive outlets, children can struggle to see a way out of difficult situations, whereas having some strategies that are ready to go means that we can help children to better self-regulate and ultimately become more resilient.

Schools and Maslow

We understand the amount of work that staff working in schools must do, and so the strategies in this book are designed to help children to be in the best place to learn and ultimately create less work in the long run. Another visual we share with schools during our mental health awareness sessions is what Maslow's model looks like when it's applied to schools. We include the same number of layers, but instead of 'basic needs' at the bottom, we replace this with safeguarding responsibilities. As schools, we have an essential role in safeguarding children and if their basic needs aren't being met then we are failing them. Above safeguarding should come the layer of 'feeling safe, happy and part of a school'. It is important to reflect on how you do this for each child and what strategies you have in place. When we feel unsafe, we react in different ways and if we want children to become more resilient, a consistent safe approach is needed in schools.

Above this section we should consider how we help children build friendships, our strategies for helping them stay in class, how we promote communication and resources to support completing work activities. Only once these sections are filled can we look at the next section, titled 'reaching their potential', before adding another layer at the top which is all about moving on. School should be a fantastic part of a child's life, but not the only good part, which is why getting the layers right before children move on from education is so important. You could display this model in your staff-room to complement the original Maslow model which you hopefully have in your classrooms.

Useful links

Below are a few useful links that I have either used personally within my own teaching or have used to help write this book. Being in a classroom myself, I fully appreciate that time is precious, so the list is short enough not to be overwhelming. Of course, there are many more resources available.

Autism

Scott, L. & Westcott, R. (2019) Can You See Me?: A powerful story of autism, empathy and kindness. Scholastic

Timmens, S. & Gray, C. (2016) Successful Social Stories for Young Children with Autism: Growing Up with Social Stories. Jessica Kingsley.

Vermeulen, P. (2012) Autism as Context Blindness. Autism Asperger Publishing.

https://actforautism.co.uk/

https://www.autism.org.uk/

https://www.autismeducationtrust.org.uk/

https://www.autismspeaks.org/

https://nationalautismassociation.org/

https://nationalautismresources.com/the-picture-exchange-communication-system-pecs/

https://salda.org.au/wp-content/uploads/2019/03/SALDA-Blanks-level-of-questioning.pdf

ADHD

Kutscher, M.L. (2008) ADHD - [substitute dash for hyphen] Living without Brakes. Jessica Kingsley
https://adhdfoundation.org.uk/
https://www.adhdwise.uk/
https://chadd.org/about-adhd/tics-and-tourette-syndrome/
https://www.youngminds.org.uk/young-person/mental-health-conditions/adhd-and-mental-health/
https://www.youtube.com/watch?v=mojzN1ZNZfY
https://www.zonesofregulation.com/index.html

Mental Health

https://www.annafreud.org/

https://assets.publishing.service.gov.uk/government/uploads/system/uploads/attachment_data/file/728892/government-response-to-consultation-on-transforming-children-and-young-peoples-mental-health.pdf

https://www.attachmentleadnetwork.net/attachment-awareness-in-schools-training.php

https://www.headspace.com/

https://www.headstogether.org.uk/

https://www.kooth.com/

https://www.mentally-healthy.org/resources-collection/mental-health-continuum

https://mhfaengland.org/

https://www.mind.org.uk/

https://www.place2be.org.uk/

https://www.rethink.org/

https://www.simplypsychology.org/maslow.html

https://www.youngminds.org.uk/

The book gives advice for educators and also includes suggestions of various training sessions that we have used successfully in schools which you as a teacher can apply and use yourself.

Printed in Great Britain
by Amazon